Exploring the Deep

Chloe Rhodes

Contents

OXFORD
UNIVERSITY PRESS

Our watery world

Oceans cover 71 per cent of our planet. That means that salty water takes up about two and a half times as much space on the Earth's surface as dry land.

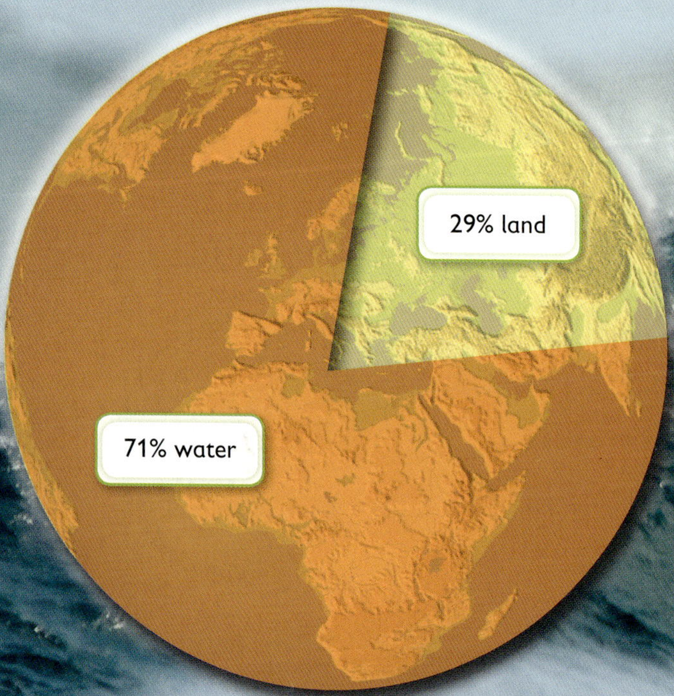

Exploring the oceans

It's hard to believe, but we know more about the surface of the moon than we do about the darkest depths of our own planet. Satellite cameras have now photographed the whole of the moon's surface and we have made detailed maps of 25 per cent of it, but so far, humans have explored only five per cent of the world's oceans.

Let's plunge in and see how deep we can go!

Fact box: Oceans of the world

Seas and oceans are very similar. They are large bodies of deep water, but seas are usually partially enclosed by land. There are five oceans in the world. The Pacific Ocean alone covers half the globe.

What's beneath the waves?

The continental shelf: At the edge of each **continent** the land stretches on into the sea before dropping away to the deep ocean floor. The shelf can extend to around 60 kilometres from the shore.

The continental slope: Where the continental shelf ends there is a steep slope leading down about 3700 metres until it reaches the deep ocean floor.

Seamounts: These are underwater mountain ranges that rise up from the ocean floor. They can reach up to 2500 metres high, and some even break through the surface of the water to form islands.

The deep ocean floor: This is the deep, flat bottom of the ocean, also known as the *abyssal plain*. It is usually between 4 and 5.5 kilometres deep.

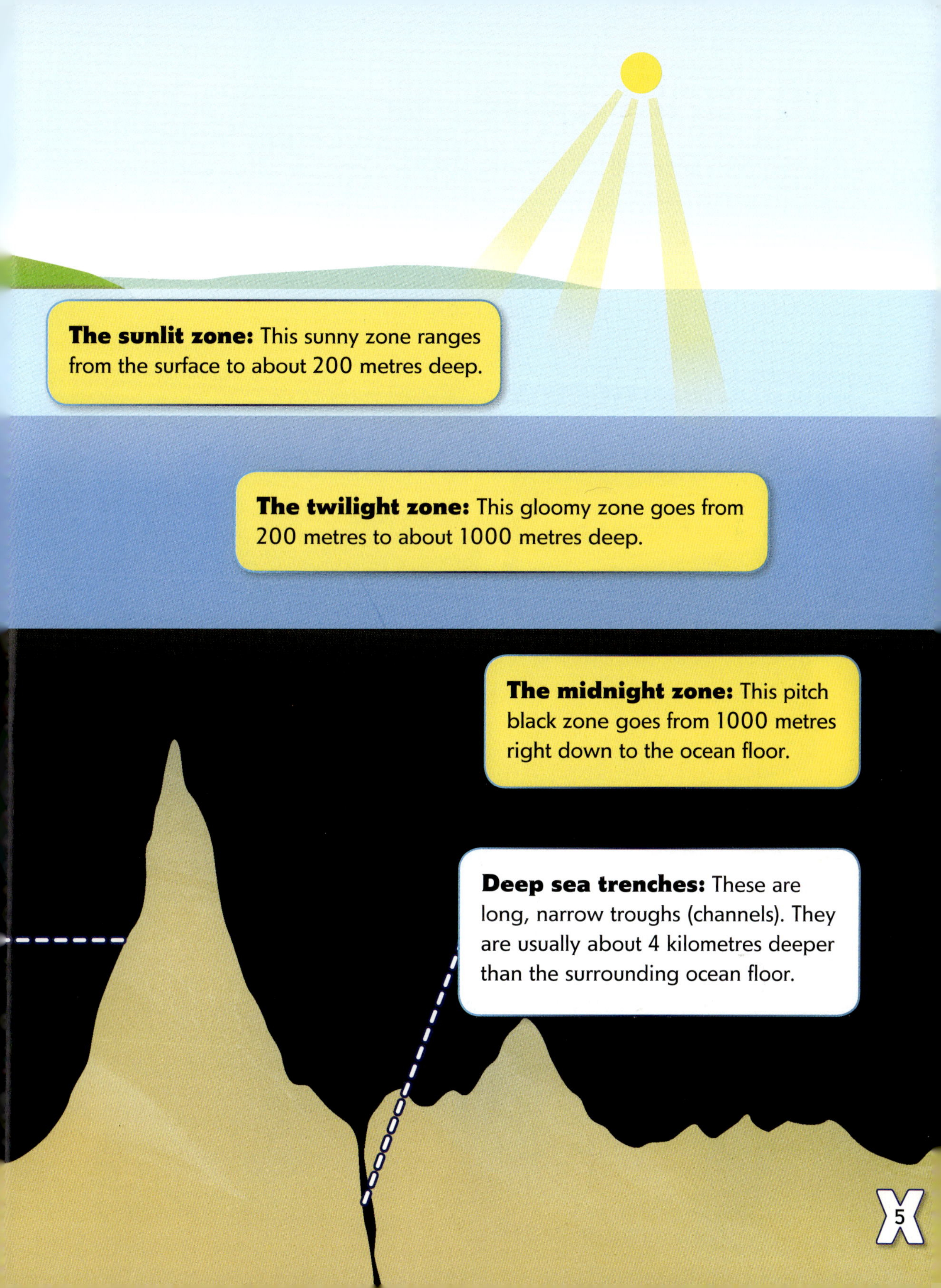

The sunlit zone: This sunny zone ranges from the surface to about 200 metres deep.

The twilight zone: This gloomy zone goes from 200 metres to about 1000 metres deep.

The midnight zone: This pitch black zone goes from 1000 metres right down to the ocean floor.

Deep sea trenches: These are long, narrow troughs (channels). They are usually about 4 kilometres deeper than the surrounding ocean floor.

The sunlit zone

About 90 per cent of all life in the ocean lives in the shallow, sunlit waters from the surface to roughly 200 metres down. **Coral** reefs form in waters where the temperature is not too cold. They become home to huge numbers of fish and sea creatures. We can explore this zone using scuba diving equipment (see page 8).

Life at these depths

Parrot fish

Habitat: The shallow coral reefs in warm **climates**

Size: 30–120 centimetres long

Diet: **Algae** from inside the coral. Parrot fish peck at the coral with their beak-like mouths and chew it up to reach the algae living inside.

Special skills: At night some parrot fish cover themselves in a clear coating of **mucus**, which masks their scent and stops **predators** from sniffing them out.

Box jellyfish

Habitat: Sheltered inlets and in warm shallow waters near beaches in Australia and in some parts of the Pacific Ocean

Size: Up to 3 metres long

Diet: Fish and shrimp

Special skills: This is one of the world's most **venomous** creatures. Their stings can kill a human. They have up to 15 long tentacles with about 5000 stinging cells on each.

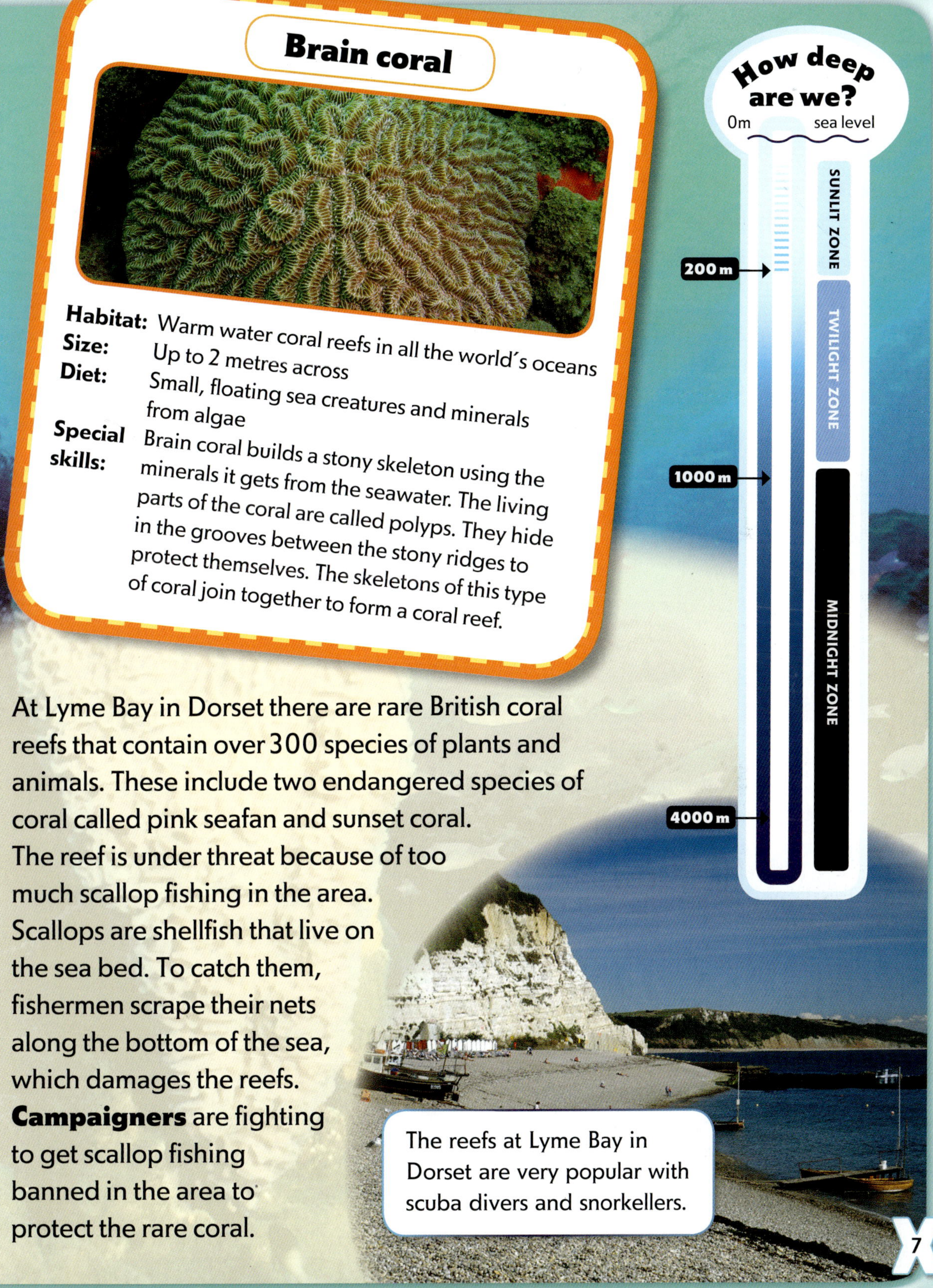

Brain coral

Habitat: Warm water coral reefs in all the world's oceans

Size: Up to 2 metres across

Diet: Small, floating sea creatures and minerals from algae

Special skills: Brain coral builds a stony skeleton using the minerals it gets from the seawater. The living parts of the coral are called polyps. They hide in the grooves between the stony ridges to protect themselves. The skeletons of this type of coral join together to form a coral reef.

At Lyme Bay in Dorset there are rare British coral reefs that contain over 300 species of plants and animals. These include two endangered species of coral called pink seafan and sunset coral. The reef is under threat because of too much scallop fishing in the area. Scallops are shellfish that live on the sea bed. To catch them, fishermen scrape their nets along the bottom of the sea, which damages the reefs. **Campaigners** are fighting to get scallop fishing banned in the area to protect the rare coral.

The reefs at Lyme Bay in Dorset are very popular with scuba divers and snorkellers.

Diving the depths

We can explore the top layer of the sunlit zone easily by snorkelling or scuba diving. Snorkellers stay on the surface of the water and use a tube to breathe. Scuba divers use a tank filled with oxygen to help them breathe underwater.

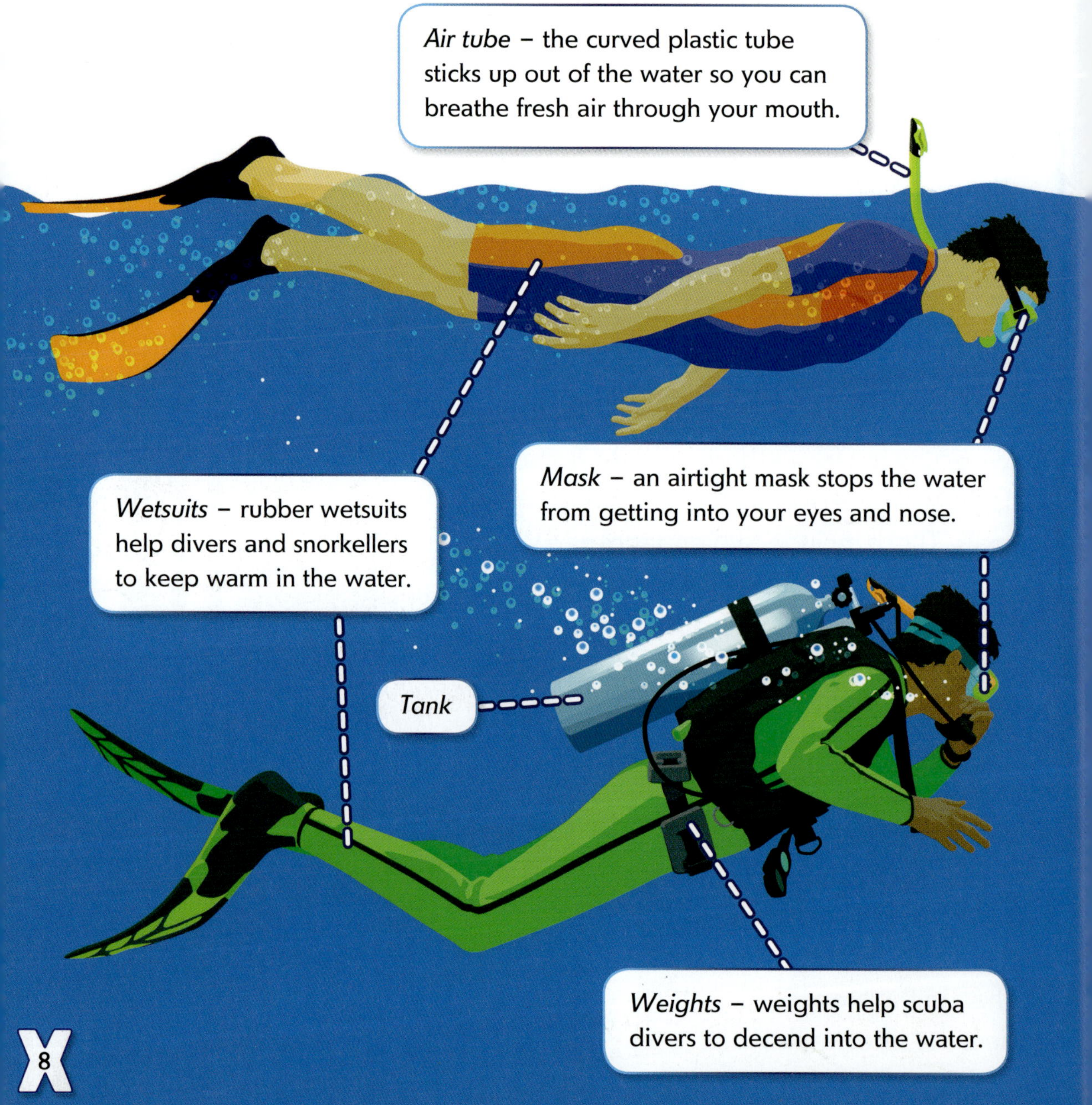

Air tube – the curved plastic tube sticks up out of the water so you can breathe fresh air through your mouth.

Mask – an airtight mask stops the water from getting into your eyes and nose.

Wetsuits – rubber wetsuits help divers and snorkellers to keep warm in the water.

Tank

Weights – weights help scuba divers to decend into the water.

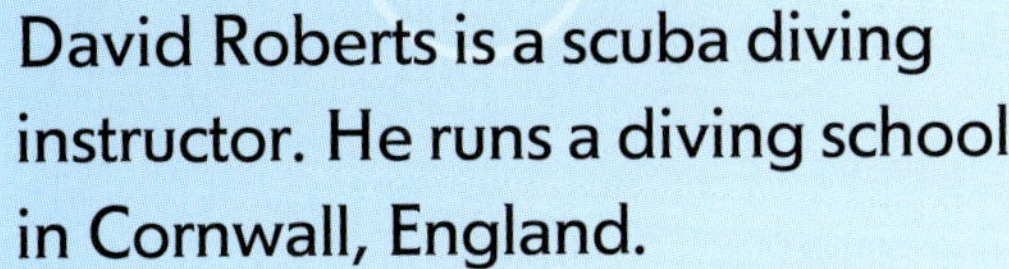

David Roberts is a scuba diving instructor. He runs a diving school in Cornwall, England.

"My favourite place to dive is off Lizard Point, the most southerly part of mainland Britain. There are some shipwrecks near Lizard Point that are really old. The *Saint Anthony* sank in 1520. It is protected by the Government so we have a special **licence** to dive there. We've found an anchor and some cannons. Every dive is fun. It's so beautiful down there and you never know what you're going to see."

Freediving

Some highly-trained divers can go much deeper than scuba divers without any breathing equipment! They are called free divers. They hold their breath and dive as deep as they can. The world record for freediving is held by an Austrian diver called Herbert Nitsch. He has reached a depth of 214 metres – that's the height of a 65-storey building. He can hold his breath for over nine minutes!

Famous shipwrecks

TITANIC

Date of sinking: 15th April, 1912
Weight: 47 071 tonnes
How it happened: The *Titanic* sank after colliding with an iceberg. The ship's lookout spotted the iceberg and raised the alarm. A sharp piece of ice under the surface of the water had torn open the ship's hull. There were not enough life boats for the passengers on board.
How many died: 1503
Wreck site: 4 kilometres under the sea on the continental slope south-east of Newfoundland, Canada.

RMS *Rhone*

Date of sinking: 29th October, 1867
Weight: 2782 tonnes
How it happened: The British steamer RMS *Rhone* carried mail, cargo and passengers. It sank off Salt Island, in the British Virgin Islands, during a huge hurricane. The captain tried to steer her out to sea but the force of the winds smashed her against the rocks.
How many died: Unknown
Wreck site: RMS *Rhone* lies in two pieces around 24 metres down just off Peter Island in the Caribbean. It is one of the best wrecks for divers to explore because coral has formed on the pieces, attracting lots of fish. The portholes, winches, boilers and the propeller are also still visible.

LUSITANIA

Date of sinking: 7th May, 1915
Weight: 30 884 tonnes
How it happened: The *Lusitania* was a luxury American liner, which was carrying passengers from New York to Liverpool when it sank. It was hit by a torpedo fired by a German U-boat (submarine). It took only 18 minutes to disappear beneath the waves.
How many died: 1198
Wreck site: 90 metres below sea level off the Old Head of Kinsale in Ireland.

MARY ROSE

Date of sinking: 19th July, 1545
Weight: 710 tonnes
How it happened: The *Mary Rose* was defending England's coast line against an army of French battleships. She came under enemy fire and turned sideways to point her guns at the French but a strong gust of wind, or possibly a heavy French cannon ball, tipped her over into the water and she sank.
How many died: 411
Wreck site: The wreck was found 12 metres below the surface of the Solent off the south coast of England. In 1982 it was raised out of the water and is now on display in *The Mary Rose Museum* in Portsmouth.

Giants of the sunlit zone

Away from the coastline in the open ocean, the sunlit zone extends down to about 200 metres below the surface. The kind of life you might find in this layer is very different to the small fish and corals you see near the shore. Many of the larger sea creatures live in this layer.

The great white shark is a fearsome predator. It has an extremely good sense of smell, which allows it to smell a drop of blood in the water from up to 5 kilometres away. It also has an extra sense which means that it can detect the slightest movement from other creatures in the water. Great whites eat: sea lions and seals, small toothed whales, otters and sea turtles. They also eat dead animals that they have found floating in the water.

The largest great white on record was 6 metres and 30 centimetres long!

The blue whale is the largest mammal that has ever lived – bigger than any of the dinosaurs! It is between 24 and 30 metres long and weighs between 100 and 150 tonnes. It is also the loudest living thing on the planet.

Blue whales make low rumbling sounds to communicate with each other. These sounds can travel more than 850 kilometres under water. Scientists have measured the noise level and found that it can reach 188 **decibels**. That's louder than a space shuttle taking off! It eats small, shrimp-like creatures called krill. In the summer feeding season, blue whales eat about 4 tonnes of krill a day.

All creatures great and small

Whale shark

Habitat: Tropical and warm oceans

Size: Up to 12 metres long, weighing almost 13 tonnes

Diet: Plankton, algae, krill and small squid

Special skills: The whale shark is the largest living fish, but unlike the great white shark, it doesn´t use its teeth to kill its **prey**. It is a filter feeder. This means it sucks in mouthfuls of water and then pushes the water out of its gills, trapping the food inside its mouth. This method allows it to save its energy and even feed when it is just floating in the water.

Phytoplankton

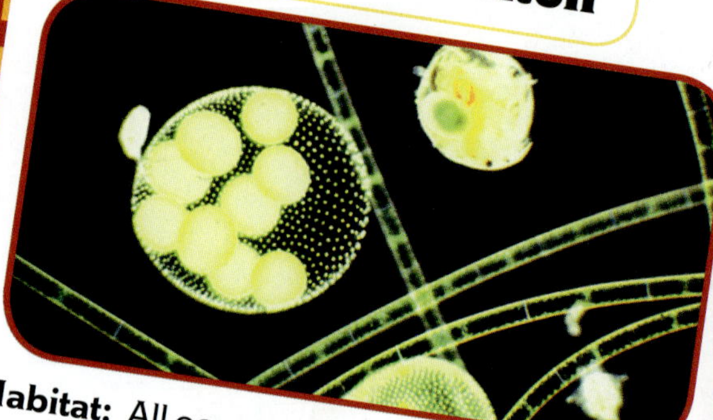

Habitat: All oceans of the world

Size: Microscopic – too small to be seen with the naked eye

Diet: Like most plants, phytoplankton gets the energy it needs from sunlight

Special skills: Phytoplankton has a very important role in supporting life on Earth. Through a process called photosynthesis, it produces much of the oxygen in the atmosphere – half of the total amount of oxygen made by all plant life. It is also the first link in the ocean food chain. This means it is eaten by small sea creatures (such as plankton), which are then eaten by larger ones (such as krill), which in turn are eaten by larger ones (such as the whale shark).

A trick of the light

Many of the larger animals that live in the sunlit zone, especially sharks, have a special **camouflage** to protect them from predators. Because there is sunlight above and darkness below, their bodies are light on the underside and dark on the top. This means that if a predator is looking down on them from above, their darker backs blend into the dark depths below. But if a predator is looking up at them towards the sunlit surface, the shark´s undersides are pale enough not to stand out against the brightly lit water.

Blacktip reef shark

The twilight zone

The next layer down is known as the twilight zone. Very little sunlight can reach these depths. The temperature is much colder – it can drop as low as 5° Celsius, and there is less oxygen in the water. This layer ranges from 180 metres to about 900 metres down – the height of 220-storey building!

Can you stand the pressure?

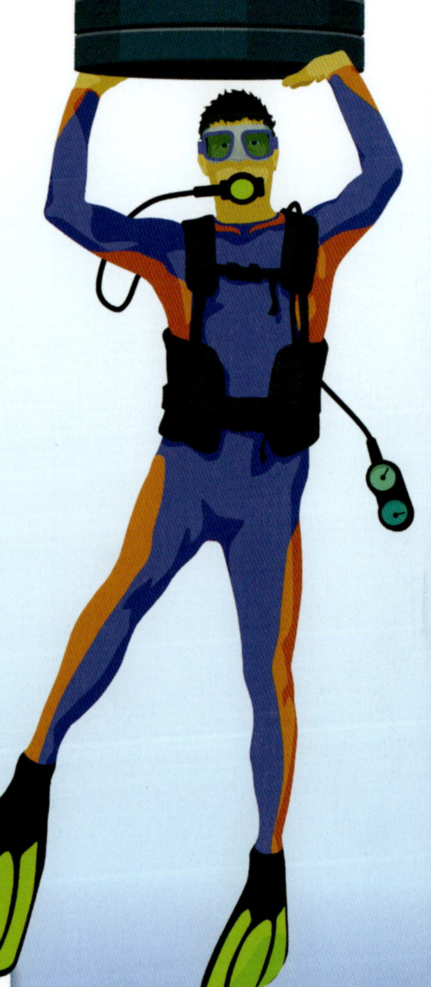

The pressure in the twilight zone is very high. This means that humans cannot dive down to the twilight zone without special equipment.

Water pressure weighs down on all the air spaces in your body. It is caused by the weight of the water above you – the more water there is over your head, the greater the pressure it puts on your body.

Tiny bubbles of air form in the blood stream when you swim in very deep water. You have to let them out slowly when you come back to the surface, otherwise it's like opening a bottle of lemonade too quickly. The bubbles fizz out too fast and you might get *the bends*. This is an illness that gives you joint pains, itching and skin rashes and makes you feel breathless and dizzy.

Water pressure is caused by the weight of the water above you, it is like holding a heavy weight.

The Jim Suit

In the twilight zone, the pressure is so great that it would crush your lungs if you tried to explore it by scuba diving. But there is a special suit that allows divers to reach it without a submarine. It's called the Jim Suit and it's named after a man called Jim Jarret, who was the first diver to test it. It's like a suit of armour for the sea, allowing divers to reach depths of up to 600 metres without the risk of getting the bends.

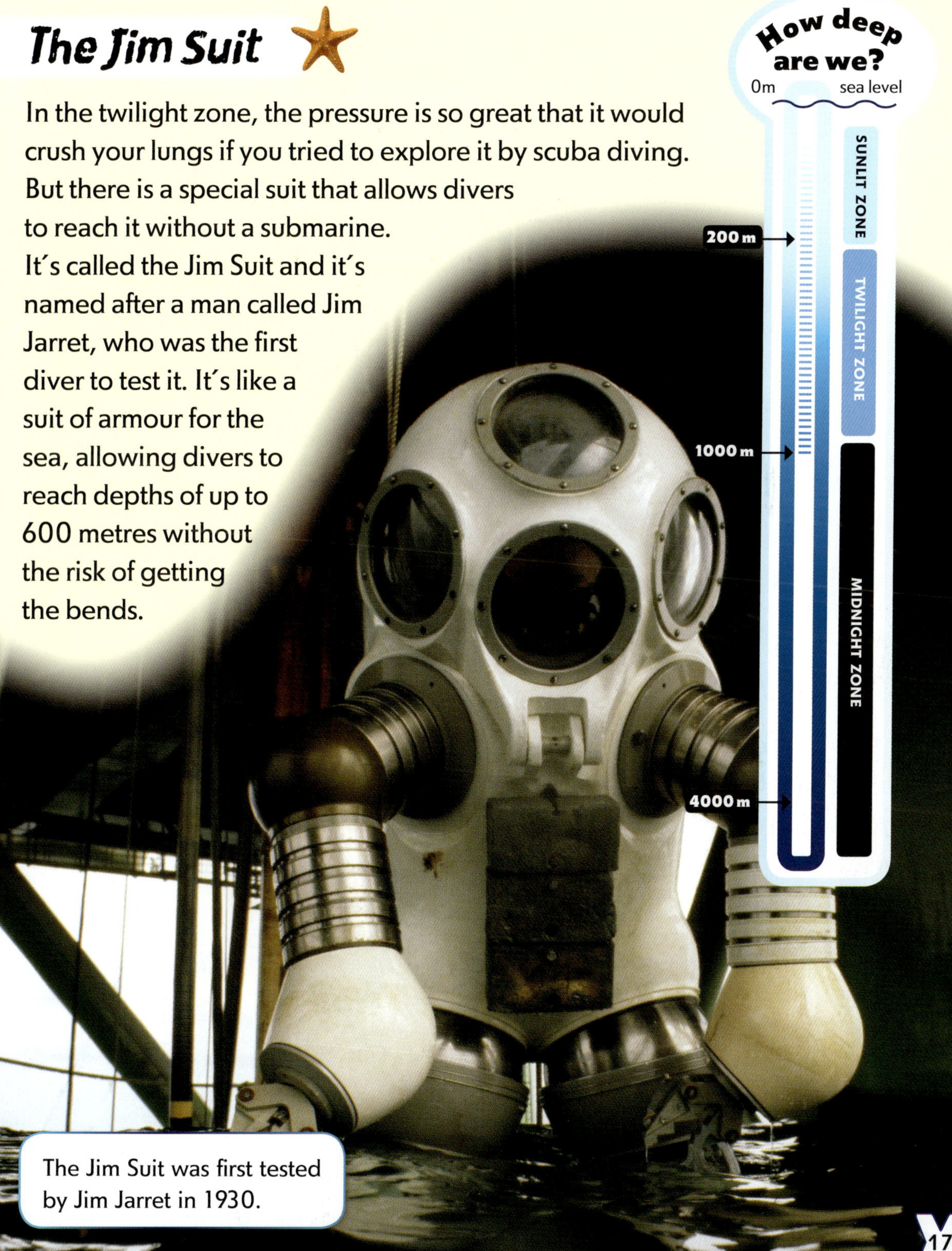

The Jim Suit was first tested by Jim Jarret in 1930.

Life in the gloom

The deep sea is one of the most unexplored areas left on the planet. In these dark waters thousands of strange and mysterious creatures have adapted to life without light.

Angler fish

Habitat: All oceans; it can reach depths of up to 2500 metres

Size: Females can be up to 90 centimetres while males are much smaller at 10–15 centimetres long.

Diet: Other deep sea fish

Special skills: The angler fish gets its name from the long, spine that hangs in front of its mouth. An ´angler´ is someone who fishes, and this spine looks like a bit like a fishing rod. The spine has a small, fleshy growth on it which glows in the dark and acts as **bait**. At these depths there isn´t enough light to see the fish´s body attached to the rod. Smaller fish swim close until they´re snapped up by the angler fish´s sharp teeth.

How do fish glow in the dark?

Without sunlight, deep sea fish have to make light of their own to catch food. They have special organs called photophores to do this. Inside these organs, chemicals mix with oxygen to make a soft, blue light. Deep sea explorers have seen huge light shows made by fish thousands of metres under the sea.

Angler fish lit by photophores.

Dragon fish

Habitat: Deep ocean waters in most tropical regions; it can reach depths of up to 1500 metres

Size: Up to 15 centimetres long

Diet: Anything they can lure

Special skills: The dragon fish has a long spine attached to its chin with a glowing light at the end. Like the angler fish it uses this light as a lure. It can flash the light on and off and wiggle it about to attract its prey.

Monsters of the deep

Another strange creature that lives in the deep is the gulper eel. It lives in depths of up to 1800 metres and grows up to 180 centimetres long. The gulper eel gets its name from its gigantic mouth. Its jaw is very loose and can open wide enough to swallow fish much bigger than itself. Its lower jaw can stretch like a pelican's to store its food, and its stomach can grow to fit these large meals.

Vampire squid

Habitat: Most tropical and temperate regions, at depths of up to 900 metres

Size: 15 centimetres long

Diet: Jellyfish and shrimp

Special skills: The vampire squid's arms are covered with sharp spikes that look like a vampire's teeth. It is also covered all over with photophores. It can turn these lights on or off. When they're off, the vampire squid is completely invisible in the dark water.

Gulper eel

Viper fish

Habitat: Tropical and temperate waters throughout the world; it can reach depths of up to 2800 metres

Size: Up to 30 centimetres long

Diet: Shrimp and small fish

Special skills: The viper fish has fangs that are so large they can´t fit inside its mouth. Instead, they curve back very close to the fish´s eyes. The viper fish swims very fast and uses these needle-like fangs to stab its prey. The force of the stab is so great that a small bone behind its head acts as a shock absorber.

Exploring the oceans

1620 A Dutch man called Cornelis Drebbel built the world's first submarine. It was made from wood and iron and had oars that stuck out of the sides.

1788 The first modern diving bell was made by the American John Smeaton. It had a hand pump and a hose to keep the air supply fresh.

1934 American biologist William Beebe built a round machine called a **bathysphere**. He was lowered into the sea by a cable and reached a depth of 923 metres.

1960 A Swiss man called Jacques Piccard descended to a depth of 10 914 metres in a submarine called *Trieste* (see opposite).

2008 Japanese scientists sent a remote-controlled **submersible** into the Japan Trench in the Pacific Ocean. A camera on board filmed fish at depths of almost 8 kilometres.

Jacques Piccard

Born: 28th July, 1922

Died: 1st November, 2008 (aged 82)

Background: Jacques's father was a famous explorer and scientist called Auguste Piccard. Auguste designed an underwater boat called *Trieste* (see opposite).

Significant event: 23rd January, 1960
Jacques Piccard and Lieutenant Don Walsh of the US Navy descended in the *Trieste* to the bottom of the deepest **gorge** on the planet. The gorge is located in the Mariana Trench in the western North Pacific Ocean (see page 30).

Depth reached: 10 914 metres

Descent time: 4 hours 48 minutes

Ascent time: 3 hours

Time spent on the bottom: 20 minutes

Outcomes:

1. They saw sea creatures at the bottom of the trench and, because of their journey, governments agreed to ban the dumping of nuclear waste in ocean trenches.
2. Piccard became a campaigner for marine conservation.
3. In the 1970s, Piccard started a foundation for the study and protection of seas and lakes.

The midnight zone

Below the twilight zone there is an even darker layer called the midnight zone. There is no light here at all and the temperature is close to freezing. Until recently, people thought that no life could exist in these pitch black waters, but using deep sea submersibles with cameras on board, scientists discovered a hidden underwater world.

Deep sea chimneys

1 In some parts of the deep ocean floor there are thin cracks called **hydrothermal vents**.

2 Sea water that runs into the vents is heated up by the molten rock just below the earth's crust.

3 The water begins to boil and it bubbles back up through the cracks. The temperature of the water coming out of these vents can be up to 360°C. Water boils at 100°C so you can imagine how hot that must be!

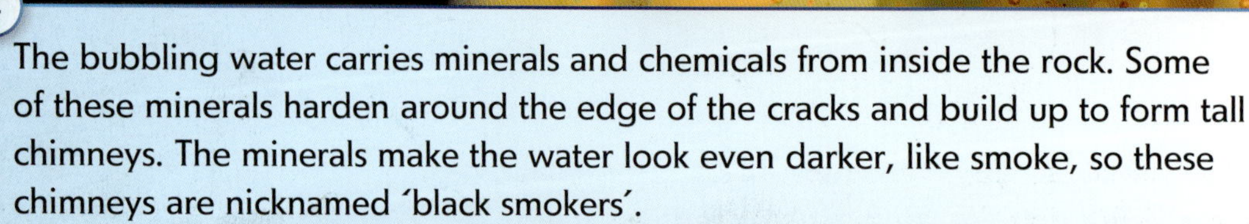

4 The bubbling water carries minerals and chemicals from inside the rock. Some of these minerals harden around the edge of the cracks and build up to form tall chimneys. The minerals make the water look even darker, like smoke, so these chimneys are nicknamed 'black smokers'.

An underwater world

On 4th December, 2000, scientists discovered the tallest mineral chimneys they had ever seen at the bottom of the Atlantic Ocean. These 60 metre high chimneys were in an area where the minerals in the rocks were white, not black, so they are much easier to see. There are about 24 white chimneys on this part of the sea bed, and the explorers who discovered them have named the area 'The Lost City'.

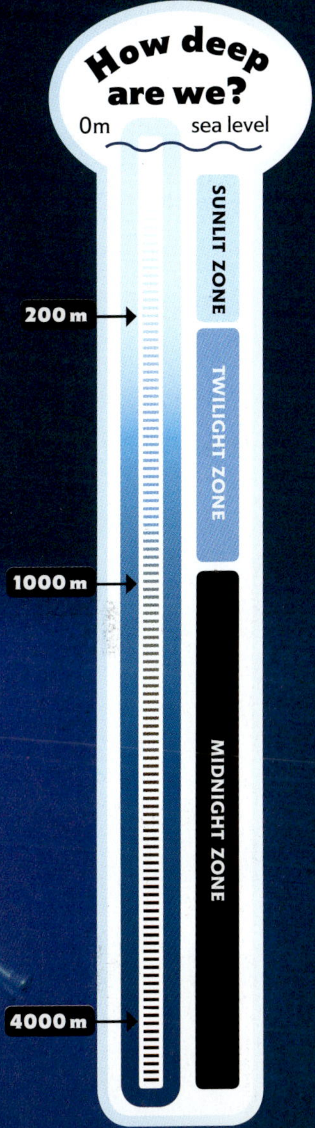

How deep are we?

0m sea level

200 m

1000 m

4000 m

SUNLIT ZONE

TWILIGHT ZONE

MIDNIGHT ZONE

ALVIN

The team of scientists who discovered the chimneys were diving in this submersible, called *Alvin*.

Life in the dark

Hydrothermal vents are home to some of the strangest forms of life on the planet. For life to exist on Earth there usually needs to be some sunlight. Even the creatures in the twilight zone depend on the light in the water above them for their energy. But here on the bottom of the deepest oceans, the vents provide the energy to support life.

The mixture of boiling water and minerals is food for a strange kind of bacteria. Small sea creatures feed on these bacteria and they in turn become food for bigger sea creatures.

crab

Giant tube worms

shrimp

A hydrothermal vent

Giant tube Worms

These are the strangest creatures living on the vents. They grow over 2 metres tall and have no mouth or eyes. They live inside a shell-like tube and feed on the bacteria that live inside their own bodies. The bacteria feed on **nutrients** that the worm produces, so the bacteria and the worm help each other to survive.

Shrimp

There are 15 species of shrimp that live around vents on different parts of the ocean floor. In the Atlantic Ocean, huge swarms of shrimp live on the rim of ´black smokers´ (see page 24). There can be as many as 30 000 shrimp per square metre. They cluster round the chimneys, eating the bacteria that grow on them. They sometimes eat parts of tube worms.

Crabs

White crabs live in lots of parts of the ocean, but they seem to like the hydrothermal vents because there is so much food around them. They are **scavengers** and eat bacteria and dead animals. One species of crab eats shrimp, mussels and tube worms. Sometimes they even eat each other.

Mountains and trenches

The ocean floor has many surprising features. The world's longest mountain range is actually at the bottom of the sea. It is called the Mid-Oceanic Ridge. It was made from **lava** erupting from the earth's crust. It is more than 56 000 kilometres long and it stretches around the planet.

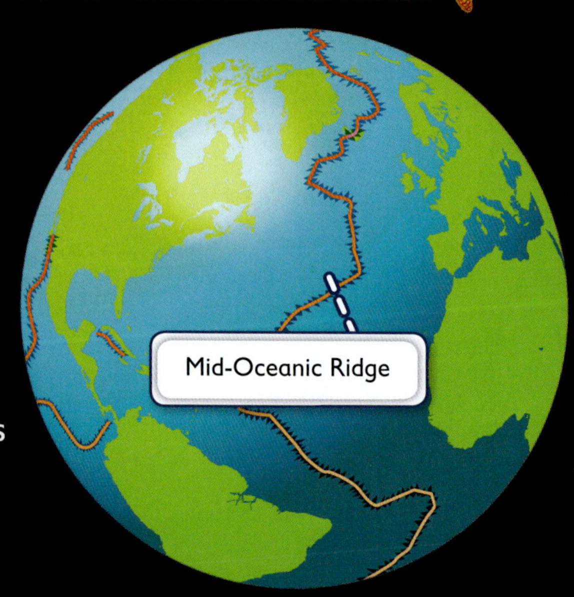

Where do you start?

Mount Everest in the Himalayas is usually said to be the world's highest mountain at 8848 metres above sea level. But if you measure from base to tip, the world's highest mountain is really Mauna Kea in Hawaii. It starts on the floor of the Pacific Ocean and rises up through the surface of the water to 10 203 metres.

8848 metres

ground/sea level

10 203 metres

below sea level

The sinking floor

Just as the ocean floor rises up to form mountains, it also sinks down into deep trenches. These trenches are the deepest layer of the ocean, stretching down from 6 000 metres below the surface to 11 000 metres, where it's too dark and cold for us even to imagine. Scientists can explore these trenches using special remote-control submarines that have cameras on board to film in the deep.

The deepest living fish

In 2008, a team of British and Japanese scientists sent a camera down into a trench in the Pacific Ocean and found the deepest ever living fish. These pale, ghost-like fish are around 30 centimetres long and feed on shrimp that live on the sea bed. A shoal of 17 of the fish were found at a depth of 7 703 metres. Alan Jamieson, a scientist from the University of Aberdeen, said: "It was an honour to see these fish. No one has ever seen fish alive at these depths before – you just never know what you are going to see when you get down there."

The deepest place on Earth

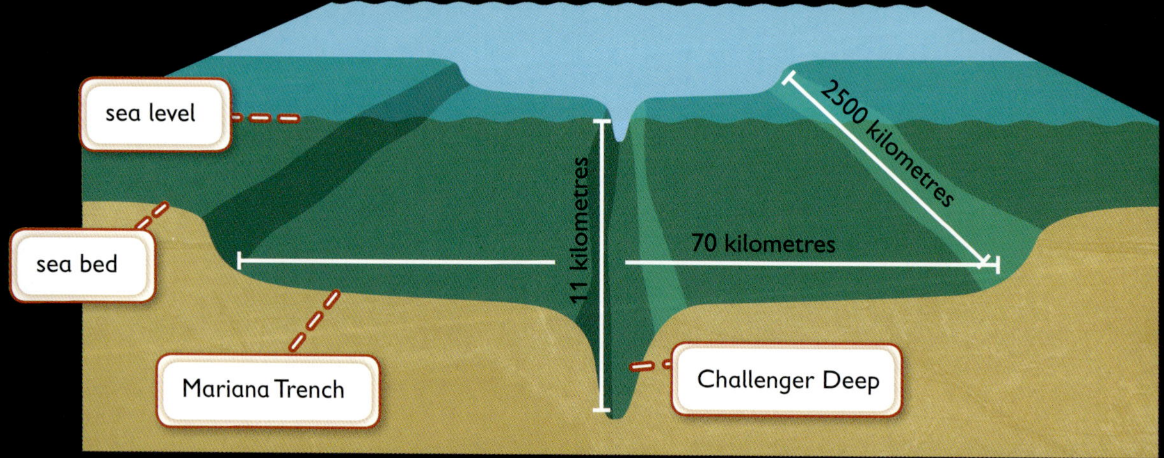

A sea trench called the Mariana Trench in the western North Pacific Ocean is the deepest known point on the planet.

The trench is 2500 kilometres long and 70 kilometres wide. At its southwestern end is the ´Challenger Deep´, a gorge which plunges to a depth of nearly 11 kilometres. If you put Mount Everest into the Challenger Deep there would still be a mile of water above it. Only one team of deep-sea explorers has ever reached the bottom of the gorge. It was a team led by the underwater adventurer Jacques Piccard (see page 23).

No human has ever visited the gorge since, but in 1995, Japanese researchers sent a camera on a probe to record what it was like. When they watched the tapes they saw sea cucumbers, shrimp and giant worms (see page 27) living in this deepest part of the planet.

Scientists are always looking for better ways to explore more of our unknown oceans. In 2015, a new submarine that can reach the deepest parts of the ocean will be ready to launch. Who knows what other life forms we might find in the murky waters of the deep?

Glossary

algae	a type of plant that grows in water and has no roots
bait	food put on the end of a fishing line to catch fish
bathysphere	a round metal chamber used for deep-sea diving
camouflage	a form of disguise, where the colouring or pattern of something makes it blend into its surroundings so that it can't be seen so easily
campaigner	someone who takes part in planned activities to raise awareness about an issue
climate	weather conditions in an area
continent	a mass of land
coral	a type of sea creature that looks like a plant. Their skeletons form coral reefs.
decibel	the unit used to measure the loudness of a sound
gorge	a deep, narrow valley
hydrothermal vent	a crack in the ocean floor that heats up the sea water that runs into it
lava	molten rock that comes from volcanoes
licence	an official permit, allowing you to do something
lookout	someone whose job it is to keep watch on the sea
mucus	moist, slimy substance
nutrient	a substance that helps you to live and grow
predator	an animal that kills or eats other animals
prey	an animal that is hunted for food
scavengers	an animal that eats the leftovers from dead animals
submersible	an underwater boat or machine
venomous	poisonous

Index